River Talk

"Rivers flow not past, but through us, tingling, vibrating, exciting every cell and fiber in our bodies, making them sing and glide."

John Muir

"The places where water comes together with other water. Those places stand out in my mind like holy places. I have a thing for this cold swift water."

Raymond Carver

First published 2024 by The Hedgehog Poetry Press,

5 Coppack House, Churchill Avenue, Clevedon. BS21 6QW

www.hedgehogpress.co.uk

ISBN: 978-1-916830-31-8

River Talk

by

Kerry Darbishire

For my mother
Kay

who raised me in her
"little shack by the river"

Contents

Spring..9

When I think of water..10

Benson's Beck..11

Adam's Dub 12

The Geography Lesson in The John Ruskin Comprehensive School –

1965 13

Swimming 14

When she was a body of water 15

That Year...16

My Mother Was a Swan 17

The Mirror 18

Wintersong 19

When I go to the river 20

Twenty Oranges 21

Loughrigg..22

River Talk 23

Sour Milk Ghyll 24

Stars 25

Portrait of Water 26

Tarn 27

Wild Ennerdale 28

The River Sprint 29

Skelwith Force 30

River Birth 31

Flood 32

Trespasser 33

Ghyll 34

The River Brathay 35

Thaw 36

Prayer of the River 37

To Be a River 38

SPRING

A whisper   among pikes and high folds   green
as bracken unfurling
I let the easterly through me   let hail melt
      into my veins
           and slipped beneath you
                let coldness touch
and sink my skin.

The smell of peat spread   I gathered my needs
from harebell   vetch   stab of thorns   picking up bold words
hunger of vixen for lambs at dawn
          both of us learning
             the bones of winter   guile of hawk
stealth of adders.

You carried me under fish-silvered moons – knife-edged
full   and sometimes shy-wrapped
         in blankets of mizzle
              clinging to juniper screes.

I drew strength veil by veil   urged on faster
down raw slopes   beating out rhythms   water
joining like paths   in drifts of kisses.
         I wore bridal gowns incredibly white   pure
            silk   rolling   silk
flowing like eels   sleeping in moss   I let blood to leeches
cradled them in my arms oblivious to what lay ahead
but held on   over harsh falls to see how far I could go until
        I reached a soft place
           beds smooth as ribbons
              marbles of air swirling wild
below the surface like a million larvae reaching up
                gasping
   aching with love.

WHEN I THINK OF WATER

I think of fern, bramble, conversations
    of kingfisher, trout, herons statued
        under bridges, clouds skimming the River Brathay,
  Rothay, and Scandale Beck. All that rain and rain
dancing away years of acid soil from gardens
    banked with snowdrops, rhododendrons
      and azaleas. I think of storms like stones
  at my childhood window,
branches and bones bouncing in currents of eel
    and perch, slowing at Halfway House, Ashley Green's
      inlets of reeds and nests hidden in mist,
  unstoppable dusk and dragonflies igniting
the cold surface. I think of The Croft at Clappersgate
– those garden parties, quartets like swan feathers
     drifting afternoon teas, and guests
  with their parasols parading the bridge to the water's edge.
I think of swimmers, Sunday-soft picnickers
    lounging on grassy banks, church bells ringing
      Brathay air, hymns and summers fishing –
  casting flies beneath beeches, ash and autumns
of reflections. I think of canoeists gliding their way
    from Skelwith Force to Borrans Park and into the mouth
      of Windermere. I think of Windermere brimmed
      with yesterday.

BENSON'S BECK

below a meadowsweet sky
     dragonflies
               hovering
          reflections
     of oak trees
leaning to admire
          their lavish leaves
               spot wishes
                    we dropped
                         like nets
                              green and new
                              into
                    the raw umber stream
                    of caddisfly
                         algae
                              larvae
                         crayfish.
     Minnows
   quivered reeds
like fingers in love
   where lazy leeches
     clung to moss
          and dusk
               passed through
          our spring-pale skin
     young
   marbled
               then.

ADAM'S DUB

You held me up when I was out of depth
    afraid to fall, to fail, be washed away.

You showed me how to move my hands in time
    like fins, to float, to skim, to hold my breath.

I trusted you like moon and stars circling
    the hollow of your arms – cool as winter skin.

You pulled me down eyes wide as a perch
    to learn by heart the silence of your bed:

mossy stones, ribboned leeches, silted skulls
    sheep bones stormed from fells and ghylls,

the drowned wild-scented voices caught in becks
    on sun-dipped evenings after school.

You taught me how to swim to swim away
    and never asked for anything.

THE GEOGRAPHY LESSON IN THE JOHN RUSKIN COMPREHENSIVE SCHOOL – 1965

– after Philip Levine

He draws a snake left to right across the blackboard.
We sigh at another hour of boredom.
Does anyone recognise this? I think of an answer
but know it's wrong. *A necklace sir, a mountain pass,* Eileen
blurts from the desk behind me. Mr Litheroe ignores her.
Andrew is doodling on the back of his exercise book
and everyone dips their heads in unknowing.

Silence pulls itself through the classroom like Sunday.
How can we know? Janet, a salmon ready to leap,
raises her hand. *A river sir!* She knew everything,
her house was full of fusty old books. *Good, but what
does it do?* We trusted her, she always got it right.
*It works the valley, follows curves, slows the flow, meanders,
avoids rocks, erodes banks taking sediment from one side*

to the other. I thought of my brother measuring
and tipping chemicals into test tubes, the liquid
of his hands coursing his bench like a magician
making something work. But how will *a meander*
help me? All I know is it's 11.45 and soon
I will be in the yard, the smell of stew drifting
over damp bicycles and heaps of spent leaves.

Beyond the grey picture window I watch rain
thunder down the fells, turning becks white –
taking the shortest route.

SWIMMING

a summer slides through an old lens
    a reflection   deep greens and umber
      my toes barely wet
         waiting for   the moment
    jewels of rain   slip of riverbed
    to enter my skin
again   and   again
    I come back to this bowl
      brimmed with birdsong   trees
        and sky   to float
    in a veil of sunlight
    gathering warmth over rocks   reeds
and moss
    to soak in fell water
      soft as a bride
        gifting me a fine-woven dress
      light as a kingfisher   a necklace of pearls
    drifting
          downstream

WHEN SHE WAS A BODY OF WATER

my mother wore the softest blossom
before she became threadbare   distant
smelling of oak roots   moss and fish

I watched her   drunk on swirl and songs
from the highest pikes   taste of fern   flesh
of sundews   vipers basking on the fell

and how on dullest Sundays she trembled on the edge
like a teenager dabbling for minnows
hiding in the shallows   waiting

for the green and blue kingfisher sky   all leaves
and wings ablur   forgetting everything
except the secret hours   marital fears she cradled

in willow-soft nights like a cygnet   shivered them
downstream with moon and stars.
I cried when she slept to forget the storms in her heart

I cried to the sound of her   falling to autumn leaves
the last swifts gone   me adrift
unable to hear her spring voice   buried

in bones of gravel   reeds and stone
when did she slip through my hands
become the widest lake   char-deep   starved

of light   skin locked-in-pale   facing age
the way a pine tree braces against the wind
and now   with all my strength   I'm skating the length of her

hungry for clouds to melt   the sun to break in

THAT YEAR

they honeymooned in the river,
drank the dawn distilled in pools,

curled leaves to their new lips,
lived off dragonflies and marigolds,

slept unarmed amongst sticklebacks on sheets
of moss until rain woke them, veiled the sky.

They learned to hold their breath long enough
to satiate hunger until hunger grew

into beautiful feathers. They stroked them
against bubbles the colour of marbles,

flirted and flicked no longer ashamed
or afraid of themselves. They rolled their feet

in afternoon light, webbed amongst reeds
and forgot where they came from but knew

they must swim on and on while their rings
shone like wind flowers. Birds unfurled their wings

watched them each evening from towering pines
chiming like wedding bells.

MY MOTHER WAS A SWAN

she didn't mate for life.
My father didn't die, divorce happened
when the nest failed.

I was the youngest of three cygnets
the one who shivered at her mute nudge
when I whispered my father's name.

She raised us on strangers – cocky
young cobs who glided through our door
loaded like galleons, gold-tongued,

flirty with their press-stud eyes as if
they could take my father's place.
I prayed for thickening clouds – a storm

to sluice them away, I tried to escape
but she kept me locked in the dark
of her wings, unanswered questions

in the turn of her neck. I found solace
in deep water until one night my soft grey clothes
spilled from my skin

and a reflection like hers floated
full and lonely as the moon.

THE MIRROR

I pass you on my landing every day
    to pick up ironing, make beds, dust cobwebs
from lamp shades, catching glimpses
    of moonlight and the remains of love
drowning in a heart-shaped lake
    dark and deep as char in Windermere.

Sometimes I sweep a soft cloth over your surface
    pitted with rain, remembering my mother
that summer smoothing her jet-thick hair into a chignon,
    her pebble-grey eyes distant as stars
on clear nights when she'd play
    Beethoven, Chopin for hours

filling the air with passion, her fingers
    swimming fast as brook lamprey
to spawning waters, oblivious to me
    creeping in late to the hallway – that frozen
in-between place I'd check my hair,
    hide love bites, the warm scent of a boy.

WINTERSONG

after *River – Joni Mitchell*

A dove flies through

swallowed by stars
    palls of wood-smoke   remains
       of an evening

that entered a young girl's dreams
    with love
       and flakes of snow stealing

          red and green from hillsides

Above   air barely breathes
    between pines gloved
       in wintersong

Below the surface   smooth as promises
    bones hide   aching
      in the darkest truth   tolling
         old age   sliding

around beds of moss
    stones   lodged   slow   deep
      as December blood in sleeping fish

The surface holds   gleams
    strings of tinsel   keeping
      then   and   now   apart

Too late to skate on   I watch it melt
    like a broken heart   finding its way
      through the years

        traces in ice

             drifting

                free

WHEN I GO TO THE RIVER

there is no judgement   no betrayal
no granite voice to sink me in this place

this bowl I slip in with the grey of clouds
and out like a candle burning.

Can you hear it   hear   a low lament
pull of darkness   storied and old?

Can you feel her song of dawn with its delicacy
gentling me down in finest lawn?   Listen

listen to white water over slate
the sling of scree   bracken   peat

her umber rhythm beating out fear   the fear
that hides behind another day lined with barbs.

This water gives me strength to say
the winter things I need to say out loud.

I'm willing to sacrifice everything   drown
to be held this way   the way a curlew

journeys back to source with courage   moving
moving   always   to her safe nesting.

TWENTY ORANGES

I could trust the river in summer when it stopped
battling rain and slowed to listen to every word
that poured from my mouth.

It swallowed my tears, laughter without
judgement, held onto nothing, hugged my skin
and went about its journey under the bridge

of eels, around boulders, through marigolds
nodding to half heard secrets in the shallows
where leeches hid.

I watched perch and minnows dart my first crush,
haul pieces of my heart into slime and gravelly
shadows. I lived on sunsets, coolness, silence

of mist settling in until one May I left
for noise, traffic, smell of street food, toasties,
tiny birds roasting on spits. I left for the sound

of bells peeling streets of Milan. Come June, heat
descended in arid waves. Thirsty for the river
times of moss, green, bubbles,

I squeezed twenty oranges and drank.

LOUGHRIGG

The lough of summer skies –
Lily tarn – her eye on wild geese,
autumn's grey beard where at the death
of a year I clung to icy waves up and all the way,
my mother yards ahead at the rigg
where we anchored to sluice the ropes
around our hearts. A fell, full sail, our ship
of sundew, fern and basking vipers,
the broken route we took daily
from here to there.

Lough – Lake/loch
Rigg – Ridge

RIVER TALK

After Raymond Carver

I'd slip across mossy rocks
to catch your intonations
clear as glass splintering morning air,

accents you taught me
before the scent of pine lifted
from your tongue, before blackbirds

and traffic spilled over the bridge.
Come autumn you'd growl open-mouthed
through the woods towards me

louder than a stream, faster than a beck
bold as a heron I'd wait on the brim.
Sometimes a rush of hungry dippers

murmured through marsh marigold edges
like angels, but I didn't need saving
I learned to measure the highs

and lows of your voice even in winter
when your lips barely moved,
and you held me like a mother

in a perfume of breathy lullabies
sinking deep into my pillow,
and I clung as if I was your child

to every word you whispered
like fog shifting from your skin.
All night I'd lie awake

listening to the sound the water made

until I was fluent.

SOUR MILK GHYLL

Easedale Cumbria

The hour sun and shadows
exchange hold over the vale,
I leave the village slate-still, roofs
      pressed in afternoon heat.

Along a burnished bracken track,
cow parsley tall as church candles,
I walk in footsteps of Collingwood,
      Wordsworth, keen scent

of cut meadows, swallows feasting
on the last meal of the day. Lightning-
blue damsels zig-zag dusk, air
      thickens with sound

and for a moment I am nothing
but a fawn thirsty for the sight of water
pouring over slabs of warm rock
      like unwanted milk.

STARS

I can speak up for my habitat
when all is cascading around me

I can stop mowing the lawn
when concrete stands in for fields

I can keep feeding the birds
when trains bulldoze hedges

I can catch rain from gutters
hold the colour green –

the summer long and when all
is parched I can recall the scent

of petrichor   bluebells   falling leaves
remember how I took them for granted

I can bring you a song thrush singing
through early morning rain

oak leaves unfurling pink
I can write a poem to save someone

I can show you a river
brimmed with stars

PORTRAIT OF WATER

Blea Tarn - Cumbria

A sable brush
slides   slant
      rain
        stipples
            the surface
              a rush
                of starlings
                            shifts   water   ruffles   sky
              from storm
      to sunlight
reeds   dart
        lamp black
                        becks
roll   Titanium white   Graphite grey
        bracken
                  spills   copper
              screes   slip   gold
to   a   bowl
      of limestone moon
            pale and singing
                  to passing clouds

perch jump
              pewter   melts   pours
          ore   and   rock   and   seams
ripple
          leaves
                scatter   skim   float
                              fells
fall
      sink

              drown

TARN

Today she is a mirror
    showing me how far

I've scrambled through steep slopes
    of bracken and scree   the streaming scars

I've left behind.   She says nothing.
    Her skin is luminous   cold   I touch it

we exchange sudden dizziness.
    She pulls me in

as if she's always been holding me
    to this journey and I have always wanted

blindness   displacement   the tearing   the burning
    sudden fight for light and air   until

I have no use for it. There is no way in   no way out
    of this bowl ribboned by ice.

Life lives and dies here.
    I'm swallowing darkness

the taste of ravens drawn from crags.
    I'm shouting   she is deaf   I am mute.

WILD ENNERDALE

I sink my hands into soil soft as moles
    threads of fungi   worms –
        soil dwellers
            weaving conversation

through leaves and seed
    loam that knows darkness
        how to survive drought   always
            thirsty for the taste of rain

                    A mistlethrush cuts the air

I breathe birch   Sitka spruce   scent of galloway –
    a herd locals call black bears   let loose to roam
        Sun splashes my back   a searchlight
            through trees   drawing spring to branches

buds waiting to unlock summer's
    soft canopy   stifling light   until
        the chill of November's
            fall of gold   smothers earth

                and birdsong

gives way to the river Liza
    wending through this steep-sided valley
        spawning arctic char   salmon   brook lamprey
        building nests in gravel and silt

The name Liza derives from the Old Norse
            meaning of light or shining

THE RIVER SPRINT

The fastest rising river in England

From gorse, bracken, earth
  peat-dark on Harter Fell
     you spring   you gather
      reel to foam white
shoulder moss-stitched shawls
  sing   whirl   dart
    like swallows nesting in the yard.

     You brush aside the valley
show the long ago
  in great blue slabs
    of fallen books –
      pages turning
by the mill
    where wood anemones

    shine like stars
      and sapling ash embroider
  the other side of shade
    where ramson
      promise their own galaxies
and gathering trees

breathe
    like ghosts at borders
grown ragged and thin
  glad of upright hazel stakes
    singled out to bind pleachers
      budding fast as melt-water
                 rising

SKELWITH FORCE

She's dreamed all summer of this moment:
    the guts to carve through earth's muscle,
veins and bone, keen as a sculptor's hands
    drawn by a harvest moon, cloud-swollen
bleeding sediment, always running with the grain.
    She's singing out her heart, hammering away
under a glassy sky. But this is the tricky part.
    A millennia of rock can be stubborn as a dam
clotted with blood-shot leaves, steadfast as a heron
    cut from grey – all day edging for trout.
Hurled deep in stone she knows it will take only hours
    to break down Aeolian deposits, silt and clay,
she has the tools to undermine roots, slice strata –
    her giddy swell notching pockets and valleys
polishing the curve of a limb to a broad sheen, working
    bridges, villages, fields and lanes to a clean body of marsh
    with a night's harsh rain.

RIVER BIRTH

That swollen summer
    the mass of you

thunder inside the night-
    heat of me   aching

to see the colour of your eyes
    heart of your mouth pressed

like a minnow to my milky skin
    your silken ears

overflowing
    with song after the storm

to kiss your nose still finned
    to darkness and musk

seeping every mossy pore
    a waterfall in my arms

a burst of marsh marigolds
    a mother

at the foot of the stream
    in a world I couldn't plan for

FLOOD

after *Storm* by Leila Chatti

A week after the deluge of siren and lights
    that raced like a stripped heart through chairs
and carpets   I knew I'd reached the same desolate place
    as everyone else trying to save themselves

in homes shaking   curtains shivering   a tempest
    turning time and tables upside down
fear sneaking in like a thief through gaps
    we didn't see.

A week after the flood   debris hauled up
    in heaps of *what ifs* and clouds limping the pain
of a bruised sky   how rain
    rained down like revenge. I should

have barricaded our lives against broken,
    I should have known a landscape
can change in a flash.

TRESPASSER

To breach banks
force the wooden gate ajar
swamp shy crocuses
swell roots struggling
in scarves of bracken
gathered from sodden fells
feel celandines tremble
at my touch   tiny throats
spilling glorious yellow
starry-eyed as I surge
like early swallows
into cellars drowned dark.
To raise tide-lines
raid homes
no longer waving
from a safe distance.
To hold the taste of glory
on my tongue.

GHYLL

I was the sound of tinkling glass
   against dark beds of rock
      I wore moons and stars   summer-long   dresses
         primrose   patterns of lizard   adder   acorn
     woven into my lush banks.   I knew my way
  through echoes
of bees   hungry fox and owls.

                          I was ice asleep in calm hands.

I was spring   and ancient   I could hide
   in hymn and healing   confide in damsels hovering
     in a splintered sky. I ran with autumn's sapling seed
        before the bruise   of mud-dark clouds
    and rain   and rain that came and went in a day.
I cleaved the valley in shifting edges

                    roots torn and tangled in the air

before I lost voice   my grip   was stripped
   of all I'd learned:
      psalms of the fell
              my calling
                    my clothes
                            my clothes
    of bees   owl   violets

                  fox   and
                     f e r n.

THE RIVER BRATHAY

Old Norse for broad river

This water runs through me. Even now
 after life away from her lush green banks.

The rush I loved and feared that taught me to float
and sink into leechy beds of moss

and old sheep bones. Distant voices
from Langdale fells, Wrynose,

Little Langdale Tarn, songs of Bleamoss,
Greenburn Beck gathered to the stillness

of Elterwater, plunge of Skelwith Force
where I played and swam the summers through – water

that healed and nearly swept me away
one wild day – a calf turned bull let loose

over the valley, filled every dyke, ditch
and drain until our cellar rattled

with forgotten furniture and my mother laughed
as if drowning was good.

I come back to this damp air, listen to her flow
of old words, early settlers among otters, heron

and marigolds, water glinting sharp as axes
pulsing the same veins of rock.

THAW

There's something about her breath
    warming the land as if she's been waiting

all winter for this moment: snow melting
    like vanilla ice cream, summer words

we scribble and hoard, silenced for too long
    in the grip of a northerly.

There's something about listening to each drip
    drip, branches glistening re-discovering themselves,

and snowdrops slicing through a forgotten place
    beneath a hedge, at the edge of a stream.

There's something about the song a river sings
    freeing itself from ice.

PRAYER OF THE RIVER

Let sky open her arms   let go all gatherings
   from mountain and sea.
      Fill my hungry mouth with clouds and rainbows
        that I may taste the stars.
Let my throat be clear   inlets flow fresh from here
   to there without fear
     without smear of poison
       skin of oil
         slurry waste.
Let new life lodge in my bed of silt and moss
   leeches I know so well. Let summer children cleanse
     and cool their evenings   and know how that feels.
Let midges dance the golden hour and mist soothe my surface.
Keep safe all that is driven from crags and tarns   all
   that lives within me   that swims   crawls   clings   hides
     and darts from side to greening side.
Let me hold eel-dark nights   full moons   give birth to mornings
   of geese and swans in sunshine and snow.
Let me linger   between   storm-wounded trees
   remember each felled branch in pools of birdsong.
     Let me carry bloated sheep with eyes and mouths ajar
       sing them down in Autumn swell.
Let me sleep each winter   month   by   month
beneath deep luminous ice
its hollow fractured light
   so I might ease from spring to ocean
     from yesterday into tomorrow.

TO BE A RIVER

to be that close   feel leeches   frogs and trout
        arrive and leave with the seasons   to have
damsels   beetles finding their way   and clouds
        in brief attendance admiring their fullness

to learn her songs drifting morning air   largo
        forte after rain   to borrow
her summer pearls   winter glitz   the way
        she dances in days of sun   nights of moons

to measure her ever-changing weight
        of fell-rain   scree   all that is thrown at her –
carcases   tree limbs   blocking her every move
        I envy the hundred-year-old bridges grown weak

at her touch   the boulders lodged in her bed
        like bodyguards at club doors   and to know
who she is after drought   the scent and ease
        in which her skin recovers after scorching sun

the way she takes hellish weather for granted   greets
        floods   holds and lets herself go   breaking banks
thick with foxglove and fern   sweeping villages
        and towns to one side   to be unafraid

                              of losing herself to the sea

ACKNOWLEDGEMENTS

My thanks to the following for publishing some of the poems in this pamphlet:

Skelwith Force first appeared in *Places of Poetry* anthology One World Publications 2020.
Twenty Oranges first appeared in *The Alchemy Spoon* 'Time' Magazine 2020
Spring – Runner up in the *Borderlines Competition* 2020
Wintersong first appeared in *Song* anthology, Grey Hen Press.
The Geography Lesson in the John Ruskin Comprehensive 1965 first appeared in *Icefloe* 'Work' Project 2021
The Mirror first appeared in Hair Raising anthology – *Nine Pens Press* 2021
To be a River. & *River Talk* first appeared in *Flight of the Dragonfly Issue 5.* 2022
Stars first appeared in *Boats Against the Current* Print Edition 2022
Portrait of Water first appeared in own pamphlet *A Window of Passing Light* – *Dempsey & Windle 2022.* & *Yaffle's Nest* anthology 2024
When she was a body of water – shortlisted in *Canterbury Poet of the Year* competition 2022.
When I Think of Water first appeared in *Voices of Windermere* 2023
Loughrigg first appeared in *Black Bough Poetry* 2023
Swimming first appeared in *Atrium* Summer 2023
Thaw first appeared in *Atrium* Winter 2023
River Talk collection was highly commended in *Fool for Poetry Chapbook* Competition 2022

Cover Painting: *Waterfall* by Stephen J. Darbishire RBA